The Quotable Dad

The Quotable Dad

COMPILED AND WITH AN INTRODUCTION BY
TONY LYONS AND NICK LYONS

Main Street
A division of Sterling Publishing Co., Inc.
New York

Library of Congress Cataloging-in-Publication Data available

10 9 8 7 6 5 4 3 2 1

Published by Main Street, a division of Sterling Publishing Co., Inc.
387 Park Avenue South, New York, NY 10016

Copyright © 2003 by Nick Lyons and Tony Lyons
Revised edition copyright © 2004 by Sterling Publishing
Distributed in Canada by Sterling Publishing
c/o Canadian Manda Group, One Atlantic Avenue, Suite 105
Toronto, Ontario, Canada M6K 3E7
Distributed in Great Britain by Chrysalis Books Group PLC
The Chrysalis Building, Bramley Road, London W10 6SP England
Distributed in Australia by Capricorn Link (Australia) Pty. Ltd.
P.O. Box 704, Windsor, NSW 2756, Australia

Manufactured in the United States of America
All rights reserved

Sterling ISBN   1-4027-1424-6

Contents

Introduction

"Being a dad is one of the oldest 'professions around,' " writes Marcus Goldman in *The Joy of Fatherhood*. And as such, it has accumulated centuries of pointed comment. We've been connected, as father and son, for nearly forty years, so we've learned *something* about this endlessly fascinating relationship. And what a happy, challenging, various, and evolving relationship it can be.

In the beginning there is a father's expectations about any new child, his first or his fifth, and then his feelings—often startlingly unexpected—about that new child. As father and child both grow older, it all keeps changing, and questions of love, admiration, delight, pride, duty, education, hopes, worries, and so much more come into play, as the worlds of father and child change. The teenage years can be demanding for both. Sons are different from daughters. Grown children bring still other issues, as the family expands to include spouses and perhaps grandchildren, and sometimes even an opportunity (as happened for us) to be in business together. And when both father and children have grown older and perhaps more reflective, there is that moment of looking back, remembering, evaluating.

Great writers of all stripes, psychologists, eminent soldiers and statesmen, and a host of others have commented on the multifaceted aspects of a father's relationship to his son or daughter, or to his own feelings, and the words have been at times wise, at times hilarious, sometimes practical and sometimes far-reaching. And so much more.

We've enjoyed collecting some of the best of these words and very much hope you enjoy—and learn from—this diverse collection of observations by and about that common but so often misunderstood state known as fatherhood.

Tony Lyons · Nick Lyons
New York City, January 2002

Being a dad is one of the oldest "professions" around.

—MARCUS JACOB GOLDMAN
THE JOY OF FATHERHOOD (2000)

———————————————————————

The Quotable Dad

1

On Becoming a Father

We wanted you so badly. We loved you before we saw you.

—PETER CAREY, "A LETTER TO OUR SON," *THE GRANTA BOOK OF THE FAMILY* (1995)

Some dads liken the impending birth of a child to the beginning of a great journey.

—MARCUS JACOB GOLDMAN, *THE JOY OF FATHERHOOD* (2000)

A baby is God's opinion that life should go on.

—CARL SANDBURG

For fathers-to-be, pregnancy also serves as a time of profound transition: nine months of mental, emotional, material, perhaps physical, and almost certainly financial preparation to become a father.

—Kevin Osborn, *The Complete Idiot's Guide to Fatherhood* (2000)

Arrange for paternity leave.

—ANNIE PIGEON, *DAD'S LITTLE INSTRUCTION BOOK*
(1995)

Many of us are not ready to be fathers when a child comes.

—JOHN L. HART, *BECOMING A FATHER* (1998)

I don't know any parents that look into the eyes of a newborn baby and say, "How can we screw this kid up?"

—RUSSELL BISHOP

I felt something impossible for me to explain in words. Then when they took her away, it hit me. I got scared all over again and began to feel giddy. Then it came to me—I was a father.

—NAT KING COLE

When Charles first saw our child Mary, he said all the proper things for a new father. He looked upon the poor little red thing and blurted, "She's more beautiful than the Brooklyn Bridge."

—HELEN HAYES

If you ever become a father, I think the strangest and strongest sensation of your life will be hearing for the first time the thin cry of your child.

—LAFCADIO HEARN (1850–1904)

. . . when my son looks up at me and breaks into his wonderful toothless smile, my eyes fill up and I know that having him is the best thing I will ever do.

—DAN GREENBERG

Men who have fought in the world's bloodiest wars . . . are apt to faint at the sight of a truly foul diaper.

—GARY D. CHRISTENSON

Blessed indeed is the man who hears many gentle voices call him father!

—LYDIA M. CHILD

There are times when parenthood seems nothing but feeding the mouth that bites you.

—PETER DE VRIES

A baby changes your dinner-party conversation from politics to poops.

—MARCUS JACOB GOLDMAN, *THE JOY OF FATHERHOOD* (2000)

The most common mistake in choosing a name comes from forgetting the fiendish tortures that kids inflict on other kids because of an unconventional name, an unfortunate set of initials, or a cute nickname that becomes less cute with each passing year.

—PETER MAYLE, *HOW TO BE A PREGNANT FATHER* (1995)

She said, "There it is. I can see your baby's head." It was you. The tip of you, the top of you. You were a new country, a planet, a star seen for the first time.

—Peter Carey, "A Letter to Our Son," *The Granta Book of the Family* (1995)

... when my mother suggested that I be known by my middle name, Halsey, my father countered: "You might as well call him Abercrombie and completely do him in."

—WILLIAM PLUMMER, *WISHING MY FATHER WELL* (2000)

"Is this kid beautiful, or is this kid beautiful?"
I always ask to hear the choices again, because
they sound *so* similar.

—PAUL REISER, *COUPLEHOOD* (1994)

Fatherhood was a mysterious state and didn't seem to become any less so with time and familiarity. At night, when I looked in on my sleeping daughters, I would feel a deep sense of improbability mingled with inadequacy.

—GEOFFREY NORMAN, *TWO FOR THE SUMMIT* (2000)

No man can possibly know what life means, what the world means, what anything means, until he has a child and loves it.

—LAFCADIO HEARN (1850–1904)

The child had every toy his father wanted.

—ROBERT C. WHITTEN

When dealing with a two-year-old in the midst of a tantrum, fathers need to be particularly watchful about the tendency to need to feel victorious.

—DR. KYLE PRUETT (QUOTED IN *DADS*, June/July 2000)

The best way to evaluate—and fine-tune—your childproofing efforts is to get down on your hands and knees and do a test run. Anything you can reach, your child can reach.

—KEVIN OSBORN, *THE COMPLETE IDIOT'S GUIDE TO FATHERHOOD* (2000)

You look in the mirror and see the blurry image of two dads—one is tired, withered, drained, and pale, while the other is vibrant, enthusiastic, proud, and eager to meet the next challenge.

—MARCUS JACOB GOLDMAN, *THE JOY OF FATHERHOOD* (2000)

I used to think having a dog was adequate preparation for parenthood, but I'm told they're not exactly the same—pet ownership and child rearing.

—PAUL REISER, COUPLEHOOD (1994)

. . . when I looked at you first I saw not your mother and me, but your two grandfathers . . . and, as my father, whom I loved a great deal, had died the year before, I was moved to see that here, in you, he was alive.

—PETER CAREY, "A LETTER TO OUR SON," *THE GRANTA BOOK OF THE FAMILY* (1995)

2

Being a Better Father

You know the only people who are always sure about the proper way to raise children? Those who've never had any.

—BILL COSBY, *FATHERHOOD*

It is easier for a father to have children than for children to have a real father.

—POPE JOHN XXIII

I was the same kind of father as I was a harpist—
I played by ear.

—HARPO MARX

Fathers, like mothers, are not born. Men grow into fathers—and fathering is a very important stage in their development.

—DAVID M. GOTTESMAN

Fathers are pals nowadays because they don't have the guts to be fathers.

—H. JACKSON BROWNE'S DAD, AS QUOTED IN
A FATHER'S BOOK OF WISDOM (1988)

If the statistics are true, by the time the average American youngster is six, he will spend more time watching television than he will spend talking to his father in his lifetime.

—DR. JAMES DOBSON, *CHILDREN AT RISK*

The most important thing a father can do for his children is to love their mother.

—THEODORE HESBURGH

To be a successful father . . . there's one absolute rule: when you have a kid, don't look at it for the first two years.

—ERNEST HEMINGWAY

Hug.

—ANNIE PIGEON, *DAD'S LITTLE INSTRUCTION BOOK* (1995)

I cannot think of any need in childhood as strong as the need for a father's protection.

—SIGMUND FREUD

Ideally, they should give you a couple of "practice kids" before you have any for real. Sort of like bowling a few frames for free before you start keeping score. Let you warm up.

—PAUL REISER, COUPLEHOOD (1994)

I have found the best way to give advice to your children is to find out what they want and then advise them to do it.

—HARRY S TRUMAN

The father is always a Republican toward his son, and his mother's always a Democrat.

—ROBERT FROST

Unfortunately, children don't come already trained, and whether we like it or not, they will sometimes develop habits and attitudes which we need to train them out of!

—IAN GRANT, *FATHERS WHO DARE TO WIN* (1999)

My father didn't tell me how to live; he lived, and let me watch him do it.

—CLARENCE KELLAND

I only wanted him to say he loved me.

—RUSSELL CHATHAM

He that does not bring up his son to some honest calling and employment brings him up to be a thief.

—JEWISH PROVERB

A truly great man never puts away the simplicity of a child.

—CONFUCIUS

I am determined to be involved in my children's lives because of my sorrow over my relationship with my father.

—WILLIAM PLUMMER, *WISHING MY FATHER WELL* (2000)

My son is seven years old. I am fifty-four. It has taken me a great many years to reach that age. I am more respected in the community, I am stronger, I am more intelligent and I think I am better than he is. I don't want to be his pal, I want to be a father.

—CLIFTON FADIMAN

My children give me the gift of stepping out of the daily ordinariness into the father zone—a place where my innate curiosity, sense of adventure, and love of a weekend gets rediscovered.

—JEFF STONE, "CONFESSIONS OF A WEEKEND DAD" (*DADS*, JUNE/JULY 2000)

Father of fathers, make me one,
A fit example for a son.

—DOUGLAS MALLOOCH

A young man asks an older musician, "How do I get to Carnegie Hall?" To which the older man answers, "Practice, my son, practice." You can say the same for fatherhood.

—JEAN MARZOLLO, *FATHERS AND BABIES* (1993)

Parents should sit tall in the saddle and look upon their troops with a noble and benevolent and extremely nearsighted gaze.

—GARRISON KEILLOR

Let us teach them not only to do virtuously, but to excel. To excel they must be taught to be steady, active, and industrious.

—JOHN ADAMS, TO HIS WIFE ABIGAIL

By profession I am a soldier and take great pride in that fact, but I am also prouder, infinitely prouder, to be a father. A soldier destroys in order to build; the father only builds, never destroys.

—DOUGLAS MACARTHUR, *REMINISCENCES* (1964)

It takes time to be a good father. It takes effort—
trying, failing, and trying again.

—TIM HANSEL, AS QUOTED IN *DAD'S APPRECIATION
BOOK OF WIT AND WISDOM* (1996)

Fathers, provoke not your children to anger, lest they be discouraged.

—*THE HOLY BIBLE*, COLOSSIANS 3:20

One father is more than a hundred school-masters.

—GEORGE HERBERT (1593–1633)

Govern a family as you would cook a small fish—
very gently.

  —CHINESE PROVERB

I grew up thinking my parents knew everything. I'm sure they didn't, but at least they were smart enough to fake it. I don't even know how to do that yet.

—PAUL REISER, *COUPLEHOOD* (1994)

To show a child what once delighted you, to find the child's delight added to your own so that there is now a double delight seen in the glow of trust and affection, this is happiness.

—J. B. PRIESTLEY (1894–1984)

Fatherhood was full-time work for Dad. When I was about ten, I took up the clarinet. Instead of buying me a metronome and sending me off to a soundproof room to squeak my way through the scales, he sat with me and beat time against the arm of his chair with his pipe.

—WILLIAM G. TAPPLY, *SPORTSMAN'S LEGACY* (1993)

Never raise your hand to your child; it leaves your midsection unprotected.

—ROBERT ORBEN

The lone father is not a strong father. Fathering is a difficult and perilous journey and is done well with the help of other men.

—JOHN L. HART, *BECOMING A FATHER* (1998)

Raising children is part joy and part guerrilla warfare.

—ED ASNER

The American father ... passes his life entirely on Wall Street and communicates with his family once a month by means of a telegram in cipher.

—OSCAR WILDE

The fundamental defect of fathers is that they want their children to be a credit to them.

—BERTRAND RUSSELL

If the new American father feels bewildered and even defeated, let him take comfort from the fact that whatever he does in any fathering situation has a fifty percent chance of being right.

—BILL COSBY

No, you can't charge them rent when they're still in grade school.

—ANNIE PIGEON, *DAD'S LITTLE INSTRUCTION BOOK* (1995)

Raising a child on a steady diet of "I am the center of the universe" is generally quite harmful. Your child is not the center of the universe and never will be.

—IAN GRANT, *FATHERS WHO DARE TO WIN* (1999)

A father is a man who is always learning to love. He knows that his love must grow and change because his children change.

—TIM HANSEL, AS QUOTED IN *DAD'S APPRECIATION BOOK OF WIT AND WISDOM* (1996)

Mostly you just have to keep plugging and keep loving—and hoping that your child forgives you according to how you loved him, judged him, forgave him, and stood watching over him as he slept, year after year.

—BEN STEIN, "MISTAKES OF THE FATHER"
(*DADS*, JUNE/JULY 2000)

3

Fathers and Daughters

The lucky man has a daughter as his first child.

—SPANISH PROVERB (QUOTED IN *TWO FOR THE SUMMIT*, GEOFFREY NORMAN, 2000)

When he saw his daughters happy he knew that he had done well.

—Honoré de Balzac, *Père Goriot*

A girl's father is the first man in her life, and probably the most influential.

—DAVID JEREMIAH (QUOTED IN *FATHERS WHO DARE TO WIN* BY IAN GRANT, 1999)

To her the name of father was another name for love.

—FANNY FERN

Daughters, I think, are always easier for fathers. I don't know why.

—WILLIAM PLUMMER, *WISHING MY FATHER WELL* (2000)

It no longer bothers me that I may be constantly searching for father figures; by this time, I have found several and dearly enjoyed knowing them all.

—ALICE WALKER

No daughter of mine is going to be a professional wrestler.

—BRUCE LANSKY AND K. L. JONES, *DADS SAY THE DUMBEST THINGS* (1989)

She got the good looks from her father—he's a plastic surgeon.

—GROUCHO MARX

A father is always making his baby into a little woman. And when she is a woman he turns her back again.

—ENID BAGNOLD

I didn't have to do much, if anything, to rate a hug from one of my girls.

—GEOFFREY NORMAN, *TWO FOR THE SUMMIT* (2000)

Rose was like her father for all the world . . . she was always quoting her father—in fact, we used to call her "Father says."

—A CHILDHOOD FRIEND OF ROSE KENNEDY,
QUOTED IN *ROSE* BY GAIL CAMERON (1971)

His sole pleasure was to gratify his daughters'
whims . . . Goriot raised his daughters to the rank
of angels, and so of necessity above himself.

—HONORÉ DE BALZAC, *PÈRE GORIOT*

Someday I'll be his student too—then I won't be his daughter.

—LARA (AGE 4) OF HER FATHER, A TEACHER

Nothing is dearer to an old father than a daughter. Sons have spirits of higher pitch, but they are not given to fondness.

—EURIPIDES

It isn't that I'm a weak father, it's just that she's a strong daughter.

—HENRY FONDA

When a girl reaches adolescence, she looks to her father for approval and love.

—IAN GRANT, *FATHERS WHO DARE TO WIN* (1999)

I can run the country or control Alice [his daughter]. I can't do both.

—THEODORE ROOSEVELT

. . . you want your daughters to adore you . . . without reservation and without my doing anything to deserve it, for the sheer accidental reason that I was the only man in their young lives.

—GEOFFREY NORMAN, *TWO FOR THE SUMMIT* (2000)

Many a man wishes he were strong enough to tear a telephone book in half—especially if he has a teenage daughter.

—GUY LOMBARDO

You didn't want to boast that you have scared as feckless a father as I am into chronic sleeplessness.

—ROBERT FROST, TO HIS DAUGHTER LESLEY,
QUOTED IN *THE BOOK OF FATHER'S WISDOM*, ED.
EDWARD HOFFMAN (1997)

Things not to worry about:
—Don't worry about popular opinion
—Don't worry about dolls
—Don't worry about the past

—F. SCOTT FITZGERALD, TO HIS DAUGHTER SCOTTIE

True maturity is only reached when a man realizes he has become a father figure to his daughters' girlfriends—and he accepts it.

—LARRY MCMURTRY

Tell me, my daughters,
Since now we will divest us
    Both of rule,
Interest of territory, cares of State,
Which of you shall we say doth love us most?

       —KING LEAR TO HIS THREE DAUGHTERS, IN
       KING LEAR BY WILLIAM SHAKESPEARE

All right, I'll give you fifty dollars to help pay your expenses for a couple of weeks, until you recover from this madness, but that's the last penny you'll get from me until you do something respectable.

—THOMAS HEPBURN, TO HIS DAUGHTER KATHARINE HEPBURN (QUOTED IN *FATHER KNEW BEST*, 1997)

You mustn't get aggravated when your old dad calls you his baby, because he always will think of you as just that—no matter how old or big you may get.

—HARRY S TRUMAN, TO HIS DAUGHTER MARGARET

It doesn't matter who my father was; it matters who I remember he was.

—ANNE SEXTON

We are so young when we marry—what do we know of the world or of men? Our fathers ought to think for us.

—DELPHINE TO HER FATHER IN *PÈRE GORIOT* BY HONORÉ DE BALZAC

4

Fathers and Sons

Like father, like son.

—ANONYMOUS

Build me a son, O Lord, who will be strong enough to know when he is weak, and brave enough to face himself when he is afraid, one who will be proud and unbending in honest defeat, and humble and gentle in victory.

—Douglas McArthur, "A Father's Prayer"

A boy, by the age of three years, senses that his destiny is to be a man, so he watches his father particularly—his interests, manner, speech, pleasures, his attitude toward work . . .

—BENJAMIN SPOCK AND MICHAEL B. ROTHENBERG, *DR. SPOCK'S BABY AND CHILD CARE* (1992)

'Tis a happy thing to be a father unto many sons.
—WILLIAM SHAKESPEARE, *HENRY VI*

I like my boy . . . and his utter inability to conceive why I should not leave all my nonsense, business, and writing and come to tie up his toy horse . . .

—RALPH WALDO EMERSON

I enclose $1.00. Spend it liberally, generously, carefully, judiciously, sensibly. Get from it pleasure, wisdom, health, and experience.

—EDWARD FITZGERALD, TO HIS SON
F. SCOTT FITZGERALD (QUOTED IN *FATHER KNEW BEST*, 1997)

I never got along with my dad. Kids used to come up to me and say, "My dad can beat up your dad." I'd say, "Yeah? When?"

—BILL HICKS

Like so much else between fathers and sons, playing catch was tender and tense at the same time.

—DONALD HALL

The son hopes the father will talk to him. What he really hopes is that the suit of armor that is his father will teeter once or twice, creak, and fall over . . .

—CHARLES GAINES

The child is father to the man.

—WILLIAM WORDSWORTH

John Elway is a great football player. He used to be my son. Now I'm his father.

—JACK ELWAY

If my own son, who is now ten months, came to me and said, "You promised to pay for my tuition at Harvard; how about giving me $50,000 instead to start a little business," I might think that was a good idea.

—WILLIAM BENNETT

I cheat my boys every chance I get. It makes 'em sharp.

—WILLIAM ROCKEFELLER (JOHN D.'S FATHER)

His father watched him across the gulf of years and pathos which always divide a father from his son.

—JOHN MARQUAND

If the relationship of father to son could really be reduced to biology, the earth would blaze with the glory of fathers and sons.

—JAMES BALDWIN

My father was frightened of his father, I was frightened of my father, and I am damned well going to see to it that my children are frightened of me.

—KING GEORGE V

A father is a man who expects his son to be as good a man as he meant to be.

—FRANK A. CLARK

There is nothing more common, more natural, than for fathers and sons to be strangers to each other.

—MICHAEL IGNATIEFF, "AUGUST IN MY FATHER'S HOUSE," *THE GRANTA BOOK OF THE FAMILY* (1995)

A father follows the course of his son's life and notes many things of which he has not the privilege to speak.

—WILLIAM CARLOS WILLIAMS, *THE SELECTED LETTERS OF WILLIAM CARLOS WILLIAMS* (1957)

The land of my fathers. My fathers can have it.

—DYLAN THOMAS, ON WALES

. . . it's easy to wind back thirty or forty years to other times when Dad and I have been together in the woods beside a stream. It never really mattered where we were or whether we had caught many trout or found a lot of birds. Time and place were irrelevant as long as we shared them.

—WILLIAM G. TAPPLY, *SPORTSMAN'S LEGACY* (1993)

I didn't know the full facts of life until I was seventeen. My father never talked about his work.

—MARTIN FREUD, SON OF SIGMUND FREUD

My father would have enjoyed what you have so generously said of me—and my mother would have believed it.

—LYNDON B. JOHNSON

Perhaps host and guest is really the happiest relation for father and son.

—EVELYN WAUGH

Baseball is fathers and sons playing catch, lazy and murderous, wild and controlled, the profound archaic song of birth, growth, age, and death.

—DONALD HALL

For rarely are sons similar to their fathers: most are worse, and few are better . . .

—HOMER

There must always be a struggle between a father and son, while one aims at power and the other at independence.

—SAMUEL JOHNSON

We think of our Fathers Fools, so wise we grow;
Our wiser Sons, no doubt, will think us so.

—ALEXANDER POPE

The father who does not teach his son his duties
is equally guilty with the son who neglects them.

—CONFUCIUS

I distrust any man who claims to have had a continuous friendship with his father. How did he get from fourteen to twenty-six?

—VERLYN KLINKENBORG

Fathers send their sons to college either because they went to college or because they didn't.

—L. L. HENDERSON

Any boy your age who disobeys his mother, or worries her, or is disrespectful to her—such a boy is a poor, shabby fellow; and, if you know such boys, you ought to cut their acquaintance.

—HERMAN MELVILLE, TO HIS SON MALCOLM

I am delighted to have you play football. I believe in rough, manly sports. But I do not believe in them if they degenerate into the sole end of anyone's existence.

—THEODORE ROOSEVELT, TO HIS SON THEODORE ROOSEVELT, JR.

I think the saddest day of my life was when I realized I could beat my dad at most things, and Bart experienced that at the age of four.

—HOMER J. SIMPSON

If the past cannot teach the present, and the father cannot teach the son, then history need not have bothered to go on, and the world has wasted a great deal of time.

—RUSSELL HOBAN

Never fret for an only son. The idea of failure will never occur to him.

—GEORGE BERNARD SHAW

You don't raise heroes, you raise sons. And if you treat them like sons, they'll turn out to be heroes if it's just in your own eyes.

—Walter M. Schirra, Sr.

[It was like] dealing with Dad—all give and no take.

—JOHN F. KENNEDY, AFTER MEETING WITH KHRUSHCHEV

5

Father Knows Best

What I learned is that if I don't know something, I just shrug my shoulders and admit it. Doctors don't know everything. Neither do teachers. Or dads.

—FRANK MCCOURT (QUOTED IN DADS, JUNE/JULY 2000)

The important thing, I learned from my father, was to find your own bone and sink your teeth in it.

—WILLIAM PLUMMER, *WISHING MY FATHER WELL* (2000)

"Are you lost daddy," I asked tenderly.
"Shut up," he explained.

—RING LARDNER

My father told me there's no difference between
a black snake and a white snake. They both bite.

—THURGOOD MARSHALL

Can't you practice the drums quietly?

—BRUCE LANSKY AND K. L. JONES, *DADS SAY THE DUMBEST THINGS* (1989)

My father instilled in me the attitude of prevailing. If there's a challenge, go for it. If there's a wall to break down, break it down.

—DONNY OSMOND

Manual labor to my father was not only good and decent for its own sake but, as he was given to saying, it straightened out one's thoughts.

—MARY ELLEN CHASE

Always obey your parents when they are present.

—MARK TWAIN

My father used to say, "Let them see you and not the suit. That should be secondary."

—CARY GRANT

My father had always said there are four things a child needs: plenty of love, nourishing food, regular sleep, and lots of soap and water. After that, what he needs most is some intelligent neglect.

—Ivy Baker Priest

My father, who was in politics, told me to remain a bit mysterious. It makes people wonder about you, draws them to you as we are all drawn to a mystery.

—JOE MILLS, QUOTED IN *FROM FATHER TO SON*, ALLEN APPEL (1993)

My father was very sure about certain matters pertaining to the universe. To him, all good things—trout as well as eternal salvation—come by grace and grace comes by art, and art does not come easy.

—Norman Maclean, *A River Runs Through It* (1976)

Moss Hart . . . once announced that in dealing with his children he kept one thing in mind: "We're bigger than they are, and it's our house."

—JEAN KERR, *PLEASE DON'T EAT THE DAISIES*

From my mother I learned to make pie crusts and to iron shirts. From my father I learned to catnap and to tell time without a watch.

—VERLYN KLINKENBORG

My father used to say that we must surrender our youth to purchase wisdom. What he never told me was how badly we get cheated on the exchange rate.

—MORRIS WEST

A birthday is a good time to begin anew: throwing away the old habits, as you would old clothes, and never putting them on again.

—BRONSON ALCOTT, TO HIS DAUGHTER ANNA

You're not a man until your father says you're a man.

—BURT REYNOLDS

Father taught us that opportunity and responsi-
bility go hand in hand. I think we all act on that
principle; on the basic human impulse that makes
a man want to make the best of what's in him
and what's been given him.

—LAURENCE ROCKEFELLER

Above all, I would teach him to tell the truth . . . Truth-telling, I have found, is the key to responsible citizenship. The thousands of criminals I have seen in forty years of law enforcement have had one thing in common: Every single one was a liar.

—J. Edgar Hoover, "What I Would Tell a Son"

My father gave me these hints on speech-making:
"Be sincere . . . be brief . . . be seated."

—JAMES ROOSEVELT

My father gave me the greatest gift anyone could give another person. He believed in me.

—JIM VALVANO

As a Scot and a Presbyterian, my father believed that man by nature was a mess and had fallen from an original state of grace. Somehow, I early developed the notion that he had done this by falling from a tree.

—NORMAN MACLEAN, *A RIVER RUNS THROUGH IT* (1976)

My father taught me to be independent and cocky, and free thinking, but he could not stand it if I disagreed with him.

—SARA MAITLAND

Mind you, don't go looking for fights, but if you find yourself in one, make damn sure you win.

—CLYDE MORRISON, TO HIS SON JOHN WAYNE
(QUOTED IN *FATHER KNEW BEST*, 1997)

My father taught me to work; he did not teach me to love it.

—ABRAHAM LINCOLN

When I was a kid, I used to imagine animals running under my bed. I told my dad, and he solved the problem quickly. He cut the legs off my bed.

—LOU BROCK

I'm your father, that's why.

—BRUCE LANSKY AND K. L. JONES, *DADS SAY THE DUMBEST THINGS* (1989)

I hope when you grow up you will dedicate your life to trying to work out plans to make people happy instead of making them miserable, as war does today.

—JOSEPH P. KENNEDY, TO HIS SON EDWARD, AGE 8 (1946)

This above all: to thine own self be true, and it must follow, as the night the day, thou canst not then be false to any man.

—POLONIUS, TO HIS SON LAERTES, IN *HAMLET* BY WILLIAM SHAKESPEARE

My dad has always taught me these words: care and share.

—TIGER WOODS

Dad often said, "A man that doesn't pick up a penny that's laying on the ground won't ever amount to much."

—RIC ANDERSON, QUOTED IN *FROM FATHER TO SON*, ALLEN APPEL (1993)

As you journey through [life], you will encounter all sorts of these nasty little upsets, and you will either learn to adjust yourself to them or gradually go nuts.

—GROUCHO MARX, TO HIS SON ARTHUR

I have never smoked. I have my father to thank for that.

—JIMMY CARTER, *EVERYTHING TO GAIN* (1987)

So subtle were his teachings, though, that I never knew they were his until I became a parent myself and saw my father in me as I began to shape my own children's lives.

—KENNETH BARRETT

A man's children and his garden both reflect the amount of weeding done during the growing season.

—AUTHOR UNKNOWN

The best advice ever given me was from my father. When I was a little girl, he told me, "Don't spend anything unless you have to."

—DINAH SHORE

I expect I must, in part, have developed my notion of character from watching my father struggle against the mesquite.

—LARRY MCMURTRY, *WALTER BENJAMIN AT THE DAIRY QUEEN* (1999)

. . . and while I want you to keep looking well, I think that if you spent a little more time picking up your clothes instead of leaving them on the floor, it wouldn't be necessary to have them pressed so often.

—JOSEPH P. KENNEDY, TO HIS SON JACK,
AGE 14 (1932)

Neither a borrower nor a lender be;
For loan oft loses both itself
    And friend,
And borrowing dulls the edge of husbandry.

—POLONIUS, TO HIS SON LAERTES, IN *HAMLET* BY
WILLIAM SHAKESPEARE

My father taught me that the only way you can make good at anything is to practice, and then practice some more.

—PETE ROSE

What a father says to his children is not heard by the world; but it will be heard by posterity.

—JEAN PAUL RICHTER

6

A Hard
Profession

We are given children to test us and make us more spiritual.

—GEORGE F. WILL

How children survive being brought up amazes
me.

—MALCOLM S. FORBES

Like any father, I have moments when I wonder whether I belong to the children or they belong to me.

—BOB HOPE

A father is a guy who has snapshots in his wallet where his money used to be.

—AUTHOR UNKNOWN

I feel really lucky that my children have inherited all good traits: looks, charm, wisdom, and objectivity.

—ROBERT SCOTELLARO

You don't have to deserve your mother's love.
You have to deserve your father's.

—ROBERT FROST

Remember: fatherhood is a work in progress.

—ANNIE PIGEON, *DAD'S LITTLE INSTRUCTION BOOK* (1995)

That is the thankless position of the father in the family—the provider for all, and the enemy of all.

—J. AUGUST STRINDBERG

Every parent is at some time the father of the unreturned prodigal, with nothing to do but keep his house open to hope.

—JOHN CIARDI

My father sat up all night by the open casket with the body of his son. . . . He smoked and he drank and he whispered to his son, he made him promises . . .

—JIM FERGUS, "MY FATHER'S SON,"
IN *FATHERS AND SONS*, ED. DAVID SEYBOLD (1992)

There is no good father, that's the rule. Don't lay the blame on men but on the bond of paternity, which is rotten. To beget children, nothing better; to have them, what iniquity!

—Jean-Paul Sartre

Today, while the titular head of the family may still be the father, everyone knows that he is little more than chairman, at most, of the entertainment committee.

—ASHLEY MONTAGU

Insanity is hereditary; you can get it from your children.

—SAM LEVENSON

My father the banker would shudder to see
In the back of his bank a painter to be.

—PAUL CÉZANNE

Children need models rather than critics.

—JOSEPH JOUBERT

I grew up to have my father's looks—my father's speech patterns—my father's posture—my father's walk—my father's opinions and my mother's contempt for my father.

—JULES FEIFFER

Every child . . . has a right to privacy as to its own doings and its own affairs as much as if it were its own father.

—G. B. SHAW

Fatherhood, for me, has been less a job than an unstable and surprising combination of adventure, blindman's bluff, guerrilla warfare, and crossword puzzle.

—FREDERIC F. VAN DE WATER

Reasoning with a child is fine, if you can reach the child's reason without destroying your own.

—JOHN MASON BROWN, QUOTED IN *THE BEST OF FATHER QUOTATIONS*, ED. HELEN EXLEY (1995)

Children are a poor man's riches.

—ENGLISH PROVERB

I can always count on getting one thing for Father's Day—all the bills from Mother's Day.

—MILTON BERLE

Children of the new millennium when change is likely to continue and stress will be inevitable, are going to need, more than ever, the mentoring of an available father.

—IAN GRANT, *FATHERS WHO DARE TO WIN* (1999)

All I could see was that I was going to lose him, just as my own father had lost me.
—WILLIAM PLUMMER, *WISHING MY FATHER WELL* (2000)

Fatherhood has been known to transform even the toughest and most resilient into a quivering mass.

—MARCUS JACOB GOLDMAN, *THE JOY OF FATHERHOOD* (2000)

To be happy, fathers must always be giving; it is ceaselessly giving that makes you really a father.

—GORIOT, IN PÈRE GORIOT BY HONORÉ DE BALZAC

Life doesn't come with an instruction book—
that's why we have fathers.

—H. JACKSON BROWNE'S DAD, AS QUOTED IN
A FATHER'S BOOK OF WISDOM (1988)

He felt that although his father loved their home and loved all of them, he was more lonely than the contentment of this family could help.

—JAMES AGEE

The worst misfortune that can happen to an ordinary man is to have an extraordinary father.

—AUSTIN O'MALLEY

This is the hardest truth for a father to learn: that his children are continuously growing up and moving away from him (until, of course, they move back in).

—BILL COSBY, *FATHERHOOD*

No man is responsible for his father. That is entirely his mother's affair.

—Margaret Trumbull

A king, realizing his incompetence, can either delegate or abdicate his duties. A father can do neither.

—MARLENE DIETRICH (QUOTED IN *DADS*, JUNE/JULY 2000)

Setting a good example for children takes all the fun out of middle age.

—WILLIAM FEATHER

In America there are two classes of travel—first class and with children.

—ROBERT BENCHLEY

There are three ways to get something done:
(1) Do it yourself.
(2) Hire someone to do it for you.
(3) Forbid your kids to do it.

—AUTHOR UNKNOWN

. . . if you see the challenge of fathering as the biggest victory of your life, it will be a goal worth stretching for.

—IAN GRANT, *FATHERS WHO DARE TO WIN* (1999)

Children today are tyrants. They contradict their parents, gobble their food, and tyrannize their teachers.

—SOCRATES

More than anything I had wanted to build a sturdy bridge to my son before adolescence set in. But I was afraid that instead I had merely deepened the moat around him.

—WILLIAM PLUMMER, *WISHING MY FATHER WELL* (2000)

7

Appreciating Dad

Directly after God in heaven comes papa.

—W. A. MOZART (1756–1791)

I watched a small man with thick calluses on both hands work fifteen and sixteen hours a day. I saw him once literally bleed from the bottom of his feet, a man who came here uneducated, alone, unable to speak the language, who taught me all I needed to know about faith and hard work by the simple eloquence of his example.

—MARIO CUOMO

A father is a banker provided by nature.

—FRENCH PROVERB

How true daddy's words were when he said: "All children must look after their own upbringing."

—ANNE FRANK

His values embraced family, reveled in the social mingling of the kitchen, and above all, welcomed the loving disorder of children.

—JOHN COLE

Be kind to thy father, for when thou wert young,
Who loved thee so fondly as he?
He caught the first accents that fell from thy
   tongue,
And joined in thy innocent glee.

   —MARGARET COURTNEY

When one has not had a good father, one must create one.

—FRIEDRICH NIETZSCHE

. . . my father studied cattle with the same fascination with which I study books.

—LARRY MCMURTRY, *WALTER BENJAMIN AT THE DAIRY QUEEN* (1999)

In the natural way of things, children only have a father for a few brief moments.

—HONORÉ DE BALZAC, *THE GIRL WITH THE GOLDEN EYES*

He is the stuff of which sit-coms are made.

—ANGELA CARTER, "SUGAR DADDY," *THE GRANTA BOOK OF THE FAMILY* (1995)

I talk and talk and talk, and I haven't taught people in fifty years what my father taught by example in one week.

—MARIO CUOMO

My father is my idol, so I always did everything like him. He used to work two jobs and still come home happy every night. He didn't do drugs or drink, and he wouldn't let anyone smoke in his house. Those are the rules I adopted, too.

—EARVIN "MAGIC" JOHNSON

I have spent hours kicking myself for not fighting past Dad's reserve, for not going into that cave where he lived and rooting him out.

—WILLIAM PLUMMER, *WISHING MY FATHER WELL* (2000)

'Tis happy for him, that his father was before him.

—JONATHAN SWIFT

The search for a father is a search for authority outside of yourself; you feel wraithlike, incomplete without him, in whatever form he takes.

—NICK LYONS

When I was fourteen, my father was so ignorant I could hardly stand to have the old man around. But when I got to be twenty-one, I was astonished at how much he had learned in seven years.

—MARK TWAIN

When he first thought about him it was always the eyes . . . they saw much further and much quicker than the human eye sees and they were the great gift his father had. His father saw as a bighorn ram or as an eagle sees, literally.

—ERNEST HEMINGWAY, "FATHERS AND SONS"

Middle Age
At forty-five,
What next, what next?
At every corner,
I meet my Father,
My age, still alive.

—ROBERT LOWELL

My father was a statesman. I'm a political woman.
My father was a saint. I'm not.

—Indira Gandhi

You can't compare me to my father. Our similarities are different.

—DALE BERRA, SON OF YOGI BERRA

Some day you will know that a father is much happier in his children's happiness than in his own. I cannot explain it to you: it is a feeling in your body that spreads gladness through you.

—HONORÉ DE BALZAC, *PÈRE GORIOT*

The greatest legacy a man can leave in the world is not so much a great business, but a "living" investment in the future, through loving, stable, employable and healthy children.

—IAN GRANT, *FATHERS WHO DARE TO WIN* (1999)

My father was not a failure. After all, he was the father of a president of the United States.

—HARRY S TRUMAN

. . . it took me years to recognize my father's depths, how I am sounding them still. . . . All I ever saw, growing up, was his difference from me.

—WILLIAM PLUMMER, *WISHING MY FATHER WELL* (2000)

8

The Later Years

The simplest toy, one which even the youngest child can operate, is called a grandparent.

—SAM LEVENSON

By the time a man realizes that maybe his father was right, he usually has a son who thinks he's wrong.

—CHARLES WADSWORTH

What you have inherited from your father, you must earn over again for yourselves, or it will not be yours.

—JOHANN WOLFGANG VON GOETHE

A man knows when he is growing old because he begins to look like his father.

—GABRIEL GARCÍA MÁRQUEZ

I suppose you think that persons who are as old as your father and myself are always thinking about very grave things, but I know that we are meditating the same old themes that we did when we were ten years old, only we go more gravely about it.

—H. D. THOREAU, TO ELLEN EMERSON, R. W. EMERSON'S DAUGHTER

My father died at 102. Whenever I would ask what kept him going, he'd answer, "I never worry."

—JERRY STILLER, *MARRIED TO LAUGHTER* (2000)

Nothing I've ever done has given me more joys and rewards than being a father to my five.

—BILL COSBY, *FATHERHOOD*

In peace the sons bury their fathers, but in war the fathers bury their sons.

—CROESUS

And though I know we are different, I am grateful for what I have of my father in me. It is my gift, my promise to myself and my children.

—KENNETH BARRETT

. . . my father's career and my own were not as different as I had once thought. He cattle ranched in a time he didn't like much, and I word ranched.

—LARRY MCMURTRY, *WALTER BENJAMIN AT THE DAIRY QUEEN* (1999)

Even though I hated him for dying and abandoning me, I would go to a closet in the den and take out photographs of my father when no one was home. I would stare at them, searching for a trace of myself, to see what I had that would identify me as his son.

—DAVID SEYBOLD

By the time the youngest children have learned to keep the house tidy, the oldest grandchildren are on hand to take it to pieces.

—CHRISTOPHER MORLEY

You feel completely comfortable entrusting your baby to them for long periods, which is why most grandparents flee to Florida at the earliest opportunity.

—DAVE BARRY

My son and my father. Two sons, two fathers. Yet three people. We walk behind a father's name, shoulder a father's memory. Wear another's walk, another's gait. Wait for what has happened to their bodies, the same scars, maladies, aches, to surface in ours.

—FRED D'AGUIAR, "A SON IN SHADOW"
(*HARPER'S* MAGAZINE, 1999)

There are three stages of a man's life:
1. He believes in Santa Claus.
2. He doesn't believe in Santa Claus.
3. He is Santa Claus.

—AUTHOR UNKNOWN

Every generation revolts against its fathers and makes friends with its grandfathers.

—LEWIS MUMFORD

There's one thing about children—they never go around showing snapshots of their grandparents.

—LEOPOLD FECHTNER

Grandpa, you're the handsomest man in the world, after my dad. And, Grandpa, you're the best storyteller ever.

—LARA, AGED FIVE

Grandparents range from infantile to mature, like everybody else.

—JEAN MARZOLLO, *FATHERS AND BABIES* (1993)

When I was a boy I used to do what my father wanted. Now I have to do what my boy wants. My problem is: when I am going to do what I want.

—SAM LEVENSON

One of life's greatest mysteries is how the boy who wasn't good enough to marry your daughter can be the father of the smartest grandchild in the world.

—JEWISH PROVERB

A child enters your home and for the next twenty years makes so much noise you can hardly stand it. The child departs, leaving the house so silent you think you are going mad.

—JOHN ANDREW HOLMES

I kept thinking what a wonderful old man he would have made if he had learned how, and further, I didn't think he'd ever faced up to becoming old.

—JACK HEMINGWAY, OF HIS FATHER ERNEST, IN *MISADVENTURES OF A FLY FISHERMAN* (1986)

My father always used to say that when you die, if you've got five real friends, you've had a great life.

—LEE IACOCCA

He is tender and wary with his grandson, this messenger of life and his mortality.

—MICHAEL IGNATIEFF, "AUGUST IN MY FATHER'S HOUSE," *THE GRANTA BOOK OF THE FAMILY* (1995)

You've got to do your own growing, no matter how tall your grandfather was.

—IRISH PROVERB

Dad and I never run out of things to talk about, but I am content that he and I have said everything that needs saying already. It's never been hard.

—WILLIAM G. TAPPLY, *SPORTSMAN'S LEGACY* (1993)

When you teach your son, you teach your son's son.

—THE TALMUD

MEMORIES OF DAD

MEMORIES OF DAD

MEMORIES OF DAD

_____

_____

_____

_____

_____

_____

_____

_____

_____

_____

_____

_____

_____

_____

Index